Come to Me

Robert M. Hamma

AVE MARIA PRESS
NOTRE DAME, INDIANA 46556

Robert M. Hamma has a master's degree in liturgical studies from the University of Notre Dame and is currently the editor of *Spiritual Book Associates* book club. He is the editor of *A Catechumen's Lectionary* and with his wife Kathryn is the author of a number of articles about celebrating the feasts and seasons of the liturgical year at home. Robert and Kathryn are the parents of three children.

Additional copyright acknowledgments and sources for prayers used may be found on p. 85.

International Standard Book Number: 0-87793-512-2

Library of Congress Catalog Card Number: 93-71538

Cover and text design by Katherine Robinson Coleman

Cover photograph by Justin A. Soleta

Inside photography: The Crosiers/Gene Plaisted 14; John Morgan, Jr. 76; Marilyn Nolt 22, 64; Vernon Sigl 34, 50; Justin A. Soleta 8, 38.

To my dad,

who bore his sickness

with patience and faith

Contents

Introduction

"Lord, the one you love is ill."

When Jesus' friend Lazarus became ill, his sisters Martha and Mary sent messengers to Jesus with this message. Clearly, they expected Jesus to do something. And he did, although he didn't do what they expected.

To begin with, he did not come to his friend's side immediately. The gospel of John (Chapter 11) tells us of Jesus' love for Lazarus and his sisters. "Yet when he received the news that Lazarus was sick, he stayed where he was for two more days." Although the gospel does not immediately explain the reason for this delay, we eventually see that Jesus is waiting because he has something more than a healing in mind.

When he does decide to make the journey, his disciples protest. "Teacher," they say, "just a short time ago the people there wanted to stone you; and are you planning to go back?" But because of his love for Lazarus, Jesus does go up to Bethany, ignoring the risk.

When he finally arrives, Lazarus is already dead. Mary says to him, "Lord, if you had been here, my brother would not have died." Then Jesus himself weeps, so great was his love for Lazarus.

Jesus commands the bystanders to take the stone away from the tomb. He calls to the dead man saying, "Lazarus, come out!" And Lazarus, who was dead, comes out alive.

"Lord, the one you love is ill."

You too are ill. You too are the one that Jesus loves. Sometimes during an illness it is hard to remember that fact. Sickness tends to confuse us and blur our vision. It can make us angry. It can test our faith. "Why me? Why now? Why this?" we ask. In our frustration and pain we sometimes think we're being punished for something. When our questions and prayers aren't answered we may wonder if anyone is listening.

Perhaps we can take a cue from Martha and Mary. They knew that Jesus loved their brother, and so they simply put the problem before him. Their message to Jesus is itself a prayer: *"Lord, the one you love is ill."* Their words resonate with trust and expectant faith. Their request is like that of a child who asks her mother for food: "Mom, I'm hungry," she says, trusting that her mother will feed her. Jesus' mother Mary also made a request like this at the wedding feast at Cana: "They have no wine." Mary simply trusted.

But when Jesus did not come in time to heal Lazarus, his sister Mary offered the gentle complaint: "Lord, if you had been here, my brother would not have died." Once again it is a statement of faith: "You have the power to heal." Yet it is a complaint. Just beneath the surface is the question: "Why didn't you come sooner?"

Complaining, too, can be a form of prayer especially when the complaint is made with faith. In fact, there is a long tradition in the Bible of complaining to God. The psalms are filled with laments and cries to God. "How much longer will you forget me?" Psalm 13 asks. And Psalm 22 begins: "My God, my God, why have you abandoned me?" Jesus himself utters this cry from the cross.

Mary was drawing on this venerable Jewish practice of complaining to God. Yet we see her faith when she says to Jesus: "I know that even now God will give you whatever you ask him for." In times of sickness, it is natural to tell God how we feel. Complaining can be a healthy part of that. As is often said, "If you can't complain to your friends, who can you complain to?"

Yet sometimes even complaining to God can be difficult. If we are not in the habit of praying, or if we have been estranged from God, we feel embarrassed about turning to God now.

Jesus told a story about that once—the story of the prodigal son. After running off from home and squandering his father's wealth, the wayward son sheepishly returns, hoping only to be treated like a servant. But his father has been waiting for his return. He runs out to meet his son, embraces him, and puts on him the finest clothing.

When in our illness we turn to God in prayer, God is there waiting for us. Like the father in the story, he has been watching and hoping for our return all along. When we begin to pray during illness, we are like the son who decides to go home. It is enough for us to set out on the journey. God runs out to meet us.

One of the ways God comes to meet us is in the sacrament of anointing of the sick. In this sacrament the priest anoints our forehead and hands and says these words: "May the Lord, in his love and mercy, help you with the grace of the Holy Spirit. May the Lord who frees you from sin save you and raise you up." Help, grace, forgiveness, salvation—these are what God wants to give us.

Sometimes, in his mercy, God heals us in an extraordinary way, the way he restored Lazarus to life. Sometimes God uses the skill and care of medical personnel to restore us to health. Sometimes their skill is insufficient for a total cure, or for any cure at all. These are the times when we especially need to remember God's love for us.

In these times the raising up that the sacrament speaks of is a raising up of our hearts, of our spirits. It is a deepening of trust in God, a recognition of the love God has for us. It is the gift of a faith which enables us to place ourselves in God's hands. It is the quiet expectation of the prayer of Martha and Mary: *"Lord, the one you love is ill."*

ONE

Traditional Prayers

Fear, frustration, anger, discouragement—all are common emotions when we struggle to cope with an illness. We can no more control these emotions than we can the physical pain we endure. They seem to come upon us when we least expect; they are always unwelcome.

Such emotions, combined with our weakened state, make prayer difficult. These time-honored prayers are simple ways of placing ourselves in God's presence, of uniting ourselves with the Lord Jesus.

THE LORD'S PRAYER

Our Father, who art in heaven,
hallowed be your name;
your kingdom come;
your will be done on earth as it is in heaven.
Give us this day our daily bread;
and forgive us our trespasses
as we forgive those
who trespass against us;
and lead us not into temptation,

but deliver us from evil.
For the kingdom, the power, and the
glory are yours, now and for ever. Amen.

HAIL MARY

Hail, Mary, full of grace,
the Lord is with you!
Blessed are you among women,
and blessed is the fruit of your womb, Jesus.
Holy Mary, Mother of God,
pray for us sinners,
now and at the hour of our death. Amen.

GLORY TO THE FATHER

Glory to the Father, and to the Son,
and to the Holy Spirit:
as it was in the beginning, is now,
and will be for ever. Amen.

THE APOSTLES' CREED

I believe in God, the Father almighty,
creator of heaven and earth;
and in Jesus Christ, his only son, our Lord;
who was conceived by the Holy Spirit,
born of the Virgin Mary,
suffered under Pontius Pilate,
was crucified, died, and was buried.

He descended into hell;
the third day he rose again from the dead;
He ascended into heaven,
sits at the right hand of God,
the Father Almighty;
from thence he will come to judge the living and the dead.
I believe in the Holy Spirit,
the holy catholic Church,
the communion of saints,
the forgiveness of sins,
the resurrection of the body,
and life everlasting. Amen.

HAIL, HOLY QUEEN

Hail, holy Queen, mother of mercy,
our life, our sweetness, and our hope.
To you do we cry,
poor banished children of Eve.
To you do we send up our sighs,
mourning and weeping in this vale of tears.
Turn then, most gracious advocate,
your eyes of mercy toward us,
and after this exile
show to us the blessed fruit of your womb,
Jesus.
O clement, O loving,
O sweet Virgin Mary.

THE MEMORARE

Remember, O most gracious Virgin Mary,
that never was it known
that anyone who fled to your protection,
implored your help,
or sought your intercession
was left unaided.
Inspired by this confidence, we fly unto you,
O Virgin of virgins, our Mother!
To you do we come, before you we stand,
sinful and sorrowful.
O Mother of the Word incarnate,
despise not our petitions,
but in your mercy hear and answer us. Amen.

THE ROSARY

The rosary begins with the Apostles' Creed, an Our Father, three Hail Marys and a Glory to the Father. Then the five mysteries are prayed. Each mystery consists of an Our Father, ten Hail Marys, and a Glory to the Father. While saying the words of these prayers, meditate on the event in the life of our Lord or the Blessed Mother described in each mystery. At the end of the five mysteries, pray the Hail Holy Queen.

The Joyful Mysteries

1. The Annunciation of the Angel Gabriel to Mary
2. The Visitation of Mary to Elizabeth
3. The Birth of Jesus in Bethlehem of Judea
4. The Presentation of Christ in the Temple
5. The Finding of Christ in the Temple

The Sorrowful Mysteries

1. The Agony of Jesus in the Garden of Gethsemane
2. The Scourging of Jesus at the Pillar
3. The Crowning of Jesus with Thorns
4. The Way of the Cross
5. The Crucifixion and Death of Jesus

The Glorious Mysteries

1. The Resurrection of Christ from the Dead
2. The Ascension of Christ into Heaven
3. The Gift of the Holy Spirit: Pentecost
4. The Falling Asleep and Assumption of Our Lady
5. The Coronation of Our Lady and the Glory of All the Saints

THE WAY OF THE CROSS

The Way of the Cross is prayed in the following way: Before each station say, "We adore you, O Christ, and we bless you, because by your holy cross you have redeemed the world." Then reflect on the events of each station. If you have a Bible, you may wish to read the appropriate passage. Then offer an Our Father, a Hail Mary, and a Glory to the Father.

First Station: Jesus Is Condemned to Death (Lk 23:13-24)

Second Station: Jesus Accepts His Cross (Jn 19:16-17)

Third Station: Jesus Falls the First Time

Fourth Station: Jesus Meets His Mother

Fifth Station: Simon Helps Jesus Carry the Cross (Lk 23:26)

Sixth Station: Veronica Wipes the Face of Jesus

Seventh Station: Jesus Falls the Second Time

Eighth Station: Jesus Speaks to the Weeping Women (Lk 24:27-31)

Ninth Station: Jesus Falls the Third Time

Tenth Station: Jesus Is Stripped of His Garments (Jn 19:23-24)

Eleventh Station: Jesus Is Nailed to the Cross (Lk 23:33-38)

Twelfth Station: Jesus Dies on the Cross (Lk 23:44-47)

Thirteenth Station: Jesus Is Taken Down from the Cross (Lk 23:50-53)

Fourteenth Station: The Burial of Jesus (Mt 27:59-61)

Epilogue: The Resurrection (Lk 24:1-11)

TWO

Psalms

The psalms are the ancient hymns of the people of Israel. Jesus himself prayed the psalms throughout his life. He probably knew many, if not all of them, by heart. They were an important part of Jewish prayer in which he participated, both in the synagogue in Nazareth and in the Temple in Jerusalem. The gospels tell us that Jesus spent much time in prayer, both alone and with his disciples. In these quiet moments, he must have prayed the psalms over and over again.

On the cross he twice cried out in prayer using the words of the psalms: "My God, my God, why have you forsaken me?" (Ps 22:2) and "Into your hands I commend my spirit" (Ps 31:6).

The psalms in this section have been selected because they express the varied emotions that arise during illness, from anguish to trust. Read the words slowly, praying each line. If perhaps you know a musical version of the psalm, sing it to yourself. Allow the feelings expressed by the psalmist to rise up within you, and then place them gently in God's loving hands.

Just as Jesus actually prayed these psalms, imagine him praying them with you now. Remember too that it was the Holy Spirit who inspired the original writers of these prayers, and so the Holy Spirit also prays with you now.

Psalm 23

THE GOOD SHEPHERD

The Lord is my shepherd;
there is nothing I shall want.
Fresh and green are the pastures
where he gives me repose.
Near restful waters he leads me,
to revive my drooping spirit.

He guides me along the right path;
he is true to his name.
If I should walk in the valley of darkness
no evil would I fear.
You are there with your crook and your staff;
with these you give me comfort.

You have prepared a banquet for me
in the sight of my foes.
My head you have anointed with oil;
my cup is overflowing.

Surely goodness and kindness
shall follow me
all the days of my life.
In the Lord's own house shall I dwell
for ever and ever.
—*The Grail Psalter*

Psalm 27

THE LORD IS MY LIGHT

The Lord is my light and my salvation;
whom shall I fear?
The Lord is the stronghold of my life;
of whom shall I be afraid?

One thing I asked of the Lord,
that will I seek after:
to live in the house of the Lord
all the days of my life,
to behold the beauty of the Lord
and to inquire in his temple.

Hear, O Lord, when I cry aloud,
be gracious to me and answer me!
"Come," my heart says, "seek his face!"
Your face, Lord, do I seek.
Do not hide your face from me.

I believe that I shall see the goodness of the Lord
in the land of the living.
Wait for the Lord;

be strong, and let your heart take courage;
wait for the Lord!

Ps 27:1, 4, 7-9, 13-14
—The New Revised Standard Version

Psalm 42

LONGING FOR GOD'S PRESENCE

As the deer longs for streams of water,
so my soul longs for you, O God.
My being thirsts for God, the living God.
When can I go and see the face of God?
My tears have been my food day and night,
as they ask daily, "Where is your God?"
Why are you downcast, my soul;
why do you groan within me?
Wait for God, whom I shall praise again,
my savior and my God.

Ps 42:1-4, 6
—The New American Bible (1991)

Psalm 63

THIRSTING FOR GOD

O God, you are my God, for you I long;
for you my soul is thirsting.
My body pines for you
like a dry, weary land without water.
So I gaze on you in the sanctuary
to see your strength and your glory.

For your love is better than life,
my lips will speak your praise.
So I will bless you all my life,
in your name I will lift up my hands.
My soul shall be filled as with a banquet,
my mouth shall praise you with joy.

On my bed I remember you.
On you I muse through the night
for you have been my help;
in the shadow of your wings I rejoice.
My soul clings to you;
your right hand holds me fast.

Ps 63:2-9
—The Grail Psalter

Psalm 22

A CRY OF ANGUISH AND A SONG OF PRAISE

My God, my God, why have you
abandoned me?
I have cried desperately for help,
but still it does not come.
During the day I call to you, my God,
but you do not answer;
I call at night,
but get no rest.

It was you who brought me safely through birth,

and when I was a baby, you kept me safe.
I have relied on you since the day I was born,
and you have always been my God.
Do not stay away from me!
Trouble is near,
and there is no one to help.

My strength is gone,
gone like water spilled on the ground.
All my bones are out of joint;
my heart is melted like wax.
My throat is as dry as dust,
and my tongue sticks to the roof of my mouth.
You have left me for dead in the dust.

O Lord, don't stay away from me!
Come quickly to my rescue!
I will tell my people what you have done;
I will praise you in their assembly:
"Praise him, you servants of the Lord!
Honor him, you descendants of Jacob!
Worship him, you people of Israel!
He does not neglect the poor or ignore their suffering;
he does not turn away from them,
but answers when they call for help."

Ps 22:1-2, 9-11, 14-15, 19, 22-24
—Today's English Version

Psalm 31

PRAYER IN DISTRESS

In you, O Lord, I seek refuge;
do not let me ever be put to shame;
in your righteousness deliver me.
Incline your ear to me;
rescue me speedily.
Be a rock of refuge for me,
a strong fortress to save me.
You are indeed my rock and my fortress;
for your name's sake lead me and guide me,
take me out of the net that is hidden for me,
for you are my refuge.
Into your hand I commit my spirit;
you have redeemed me, O Lord, faithful God.

Ps 31:1-5
—The New Revised Standard Version

Psalm 131

HUMBLE TRUST IN GOD

Lord, my heart is not proud;
nor are my eyes haughty.
I do not busy myself with great matters,
with things too sublime for me.
Rather, I have stilled my soul,
hushed it like a weaned child.
Like a weaned child on its mother's lap,
so is my soul within me.

Israel, hope in the Lord,
now and forever.
—*The New American Bible (1991)*

Psalm 91

GOD OUR PROTECTOR

You who dwell in the shelter of the Most High,
who abide in the shadow of the Almighty,
say: "My Refuge and my Strength,
my God in whom I trust."
For God will save you from the snare of the fowler,
from the destroying pestilence.
With pinions God will cover you,
and under God's wings you shall find refuge;
God's faithfulness is a guard and a shield.
You will not fear the terror of the night
nor the arrow that flies by day;
not the pestilence that stalks in darkness
nor the plague that destroys at noon.
Though a thousand fall at your side,
ten thousand at your right side,
you will remain secure . . .
because you have God for your refuge.
You have made the Most High your stronghold.
No harm shall befall you,
nor shall affliction come near your tent;

God has commanded angels
to guard you in all your ways.
In their hands they shall raise you up
so that you will not hurt your foot against a stone.
You shall tread upon the lion and the viper;
you shall trample the lion and the dragon.
"Because you cling to me, I will deliver you;
I will protect you because you acknowledge my name.
You shall call upon me and I will answer you.
I will be with you in times of trouble;
I will deliver you and glorify you
and will show you my salvation."

—Psalms Anew

Psalm 121

THE GUARDIAN OF ISRAEL

I lift up my eyes to the mountains;
where is my help to come from?
My help comes from Yahweh
who made heaven and earth.

May he save your foot from stumbling;
may he, your guardian, not fall asleep!
You see—he neither sleeps nor slumbers,
the guardian of Israel.

Yahweh is your guardian, your shade,
Yahweh, at your right hand.

By day the sun will not strike you,
nor the moon by night.
Yahweh guards you from all harm
Yahweh guards your life,
Yahweh guards your comings and goings,
henceforth and for ever.
—The New Jerusalem Bible

Psalm 138

IN GRATITUDE FOR HEALING

I give you thanks, O Lord,
with my whole heart;
before the gods I sing your praise;
I bow down toward your holy temple
and give thanks to your name
for your steadfast love and your faithfulness;
for you have exalted your name
and your word
above everything.
On the day I called, you answered me,
you increased my strength of soul.
The Lord will fulfill his purpose for me;
your steadfast love, O Lord, endures forever.
Do not forsake the work of your hands.
Ps 138:1-3, 8
—The New Revised Standard Version

THREE

Brief Prayers

These short prayers can be prayed from memory and coordinated with the rhythm of your breathing during those times when it is too difficult to do anything else. You may also find that praying this way helps you to relax the tension in your body, particularly around areas of pain.

Lord Jesus Christ,
Son of the Living God,
have mercy on me,
a sinner.

Jesus, mercy.

Lord have mercy,
Christ have mercy,
Lord have mercy.

Lamb of God,
you take away the sins of the world,
have mercy on me.

I adore you, O Christ, and I bless you,
because by your holy cross you have redeemed the world.

Heart of Jesus, burning with love for us,
inflame my heart with love for you.

Lord, do not abandon me.

Your will be done.

Come, Lord Jesus!

Lord, I believe;
help my unbelief.

My Lord and my God!

God, help me!

FOUR

Prayers During a Time of Illness

Of all the definitions of prayer, perhaps "speaking with God" is the simplest. We can talk to God in many ways, in our own words and in the words of others. The prayers in this section, which have been composed by a variety of people, express people's feelings and thoughts when confronting sickness. Perhaps they will help you find the right words to express your own feelings and thoughts at this time. Remember that speaking with God also involves listening. Allow for some quiet time to hear God's voice.

MORNING PRAYER

Loving God, as morning breaks, I offer you praise for the gift of life. I pray for the wisdom and strength of your Holy Spirit so that I may be ready for whatever this day will bring. Teach me to see Christ in everyone with whom I will have contact today—doctors, nurses, staff, fellow patients, family, and friends. Grant me patience in pain and the compassion to look beyond myself.

You are my strength, O Lord, I rely on you this day.

EVENING PRAYER

As daylight fades and night approaches, I long for you, O Lord. You have been with me through this day, stay near me now as darkness falls. Sustain my hope and do not let my trust weaken. Show your mercy and compassion to all who suffer.

You are my light, O Lord, when darkness surrounds me.

NIGHT PRAYER

Heavenly Father, as this day ends, I give you thanks for the quiet ways your love has been with me. Grant me peaceful sleep and let your healing Spirit be at work in me to restore me to health. I ask this in the name of Jesus, the Lord. Amen.

FOR A SLEEPLESS NIGHT

Lord, I cannot sleep. I lie awake, thinking about things and worrying. I worry about my health, my family, the future—a countless number of things. I am weary but I find no rest.

I remember your words: "Can any of you live a bit longer by worrying about it?" (Mt 6:27). Help me to take your words to heart, O Lord. Let me place each concern in your hands. Grant me peace, O Lord, and let me sleep.

IN TIME OF SICKNESS

Lord Jesus,
you suffered and died for me;
you understand suffering and you share it with us.
Teach me to accept my pains,
to bear them in union with you,
and to offer them up for the forgiveness of my sins
and for the welfare of the living and the dead.
Calm my fears, increase my trust in you;
make me patient and cooperative with those who serve me,
and if it be your will,
please restore me to health,
so that I may work for your honor and glory
and for the salvation of all.

—*Lord Hear Our Prayer*

PRAYER BEFORE SURGERY

Lord, when I think of surgery, I am anxious, but I know that through the skill you have given to my doctors and nurses, you can bring relief to my body. Be with the doctors and nurses in your power and wisdom, and be with me in your love and peace. Amen.

—St. Joseph Medical Center

PRAYER FOLLOWING SURGERY

O Lord God, you who are the greatest healer; I thank you for your watchful care over me in my hours of crisis. Help me to regain my health and be with me during my recovery. Strengthen me and keep me cheerful. Help me to bear with patience and fortitude whatever pain I may have. May I always be aware of your comforting presence and always be thankful for your divine gift of life.

—St. Joseph Medical Center

PRAYER WHEN SUFFERING PAIN

Lord God, help me to be open to what you want to do in my life through this suffering. I do not understand why I suffer, but I know that you once suffered, and that today you are with me as I suffer. I find suffering difficult and more than I can bear, so help me to rely on the truth of your word that with suffering you will provide the strength to bear it, or a way out. Help me to look forward in faith to that day when you will come to transform my lowliness into your glory.

—St. Joseph Medical Center

SERENITY PRAYER

God, grant me the serenity
to accept the things I cannot change,
the courage to change the things I can,
and the wisdom to know the difference.
—Reinhold Niebuhr

IN TIME OF SERIOUS ILLNESS

God, our Father, eternal mystery,
I believe in your boundless, unchanging love.
You have created me for yourself,
to enjoy your peace and love for all eternity.
Help me to overcome my failings,
my fear of suffering,
my dread of the unknown.
I will do all in my power to improve or regain my health,
and fulfill all the obligations of my state in life,
particularly to those nearest me.
Bring me finally to perfect union with your will.
I accept now the time, place, and manner of my death,
knowing it is but a change
to an infinitely better life with you.
Yes, Lord, I want to serve you.
Yes, I want to be with you.
—Robert L. Mutchler

IN TIME OF ILLNESS

O God, our Father, bless and help us in the illnesses which have come upon us. Give us courage and patience, endurance and cheerfulness to bear all weakness and all pain; and give us the mind at rest, which will make our recovery all the quicker.

Give to all doctors, surgeons, and nurses who attend us skill in their hands, wisdom in their minds, and gentleness and sympathy in their hearts.

Help us not to worry too much, but to leave ourselves in the hands of wise and skillful people who have the gift of healing, and in your hands.

Lord Jesus, come to us this day and at this time, and show us that your healing touch has never lost its ancient power. This we ask for your love's sake.

—*William Barclay*

PRAYER FOR STRENGTH OF SPIRIT

Sometimes, it's very hard to pray, God,
when I feel so absorbed in my pain
and in not knowing what all this means.
I can't help but ask why?
Why me?
Why now?

In searching for these answers,
I somehow feel you are near,
helping me to cope
with all the changes I experience.
Gentle God, help me to be patient.
Let me feel that in being sick
I am coming to know you better.
Let me care for me so that I may gain
Strength of spirit once again.
—*Valerie Lesniak, CSJ*

PRAYER FOR MY FAMILY

Loving God, of all the gifts you have given me, none is more precious than the love of my family. I place each one of them in your hand, trusting in your care for them. Relieve their anxieties and fears. Keep us united during this time of trial, and through it help us to know and love you more.

FOR RECOVERY FROM SICKNESS

God of heavenly power, one word from you can free us from every weakness and disease. Kindly hear our prayers, free us from our sickness, restore our health, and give us the vigor to praise you unceasingly. We ask this through Christ our Lord. Amen.
—*Gallican Liturgy (7th century)*

RAISE ME UP, LORD

Raise me up, Lord, do not abandon your servant.
I want health that I may sing to you
and help your people lead holy lives.
I plead with you:
you are my strength, do not desert me.
I have grown weak amid the storm
but I long to return to you.
—St. Gregory Nazianzen

YOUR WILL BE DONE

God and loving Father,
your will be done.
I offer my sickness with all its suffering to you,
together with all that my Savior has suffered for me.
By the power of his blessed passion,
have mercy on me
and free me from this illness and pain
if it be according to your will
and for my good.
Lord, I entrust my life and my death to you;
do with me as you please.
In sickness and in health,
I only want to love you always.
—Lord Hear Our Prayer

LORD JESUS, HEALER

Lord Jesus, healer of our souls and bodies,
during your life on earth,
you went about doing good,
healing every manner of sickness and disease,
strengthening, curing, comforting, and consoling.
You want nothing more than to see us healthy and happy.
You are the enemy of death and disease,
and in and through you they are overcome and conquered.
Lay your healing hands upon us now,
so that we may live in your praise untiringly.

—Lord Hear Our Prayer

FLOOD THE PATH WITH LIGHT

God of our life, there are days when the burdens we carry chafe our shoulders and weigh us down; when the road seems dreary and endless, the skies grey and threatening; when our lives have no music in them, and our hearts are lonely, and our souls have lost their courage. Flood the path with light, turn our eyes to where the skies are full of promise.

—St. Augustine

BEHOLD, JESUS

Behold, Jesus, the woman with the swollen breasts; the tumor on her chest is as large and red as a rose.

Behold, Jesus, the man whose eyes are blind; the eyeballs are covered with a thick shell, through which no light can pass.

Behold, Jesus, the woman bleeding; blood oozes from her body like bitter wine, staining the ground on which she walks.

Behold, Jesus, the man whose legs are wasted; they are like two spindly sticks, which crack when he crawls.

Pluck the rose, dissolve the shells, staunch the flow, strengthen the sticks, that all may reflect your glory.

—Celtic Prayer

PRAYER ON RECOVERY FROM ILLNESS

My God, my heart is full of thankfulness to you. You were with me in my sorrow and have restored me to health and happiness. Give me now the moral strength to fulfill the good resolutions that were in my heart when I was ill. May I be mindful of the love that was given me by those whose hearts were burdened with anxiety as I was. Grant that I may be ever mindful of my gratitude toward them. May I in my gratitude serve you with a loving heart. Blessed are you, eternally our God, ruler of the universe, who have blessed me with life and restored me to well-being and happiness.

—*St. Joseph Medical Center*

FIVE

Sacramental Moments

Sacraments are often called encounters with Christ. They provide us with special opportunities to meet Christ, to experience his presence. The sacraments are indeed privileged moments of Jesus' presence to us—moments of comfort, forgiveness, healing, and communion.

Christ is also present in the people who minister the sacraments to us, priests, deacons, or lay ministers. During an illness we are often cut off from our family and friends and the minister of the sick is usually a welcome visitor. His or her presence is a sign of the presence of Christ who cares for us.

The ministers of the sacraments also represent the people who sent them to us. The prayers of our parish, indeed of the whole church, are with us during this time. The sacraments we share are tangible signs of the unity we share with the church. Our prayers and suffering during an illness can be offered for the good of the whole church.

The sacraments most frequently celebrated

with the sick are reconciliation, communion, anointing of the sick, and viaticum. The prayers in this section will help us to prepare for these sacramental moments and to reflect on them afterward.

RECONCILIATION

The celebration of reconciliation during a time of illness can be very comforting. It is an opportunity to let go of past sins and failings which can be so burdensome. It is a chance to be free from guilt and to understand that Christ loves and accepts us just as we are.

The sacrament of reconciliation can also foster our healing. When our hearts are at peace with God, our bodies can sometimes recover more speedily. When past hurts are forgiven and broken relationships mended, we recognize that our suffering can indeed work for the good.

Prayer for Openness

Lord, you are merciful and kind. Look on me with compassion as I turn to you. Help me to recognize my sins and to turn away from them. Give me the strength and courage to accept your forgiveness and to live according to your word. Amen.

Scripture

When the Pharisees heard that Jesus had silenced the Sadducees, they came together, and one of them, a teacher of the Law, tried to trap him with a question. "Teacher," he asked, "which is the greatest commandment in the Law?"

Jesus answered, "'Love the Lord your God with all your heart, with all your soul, and with all your mind.' This is the greatest and the most important commandment. The second most important commandment is like it: 'Love your neighbor as you love yourself.' The whole Law of Moses and the teachings of the prophets depend on these two commandments" (Mt 22:34-40).

(You may wish to choose a different scripture reading from Chapter 6 in this book.)

Examination of Conscience

The questions below are one way to examine yourself in preparation for the sacrament of reconciliation. You may also wish to use some other more familiar means, such as the ten commandments.

Do I love God with all my heart and all my strength?

How have I failed to love God?

What has been my attitude toward God during this illness?

How have I failed to love my neighbor?

Which of my relationships requires some reconciliation or forgiveness on my part?

What has been my attitude toward others during this time of illness?

Act of Contrition

My God,
I am sorry for my sins with all my heart.
In choosing to do wrong
and failing to do good,
I have sinned against you
whom I should love above all things.
I firmly intend, with your help,
to do penance,
to sin no more,
and to avoid whatever leads me to sin.
Our Savior Jesus Christ
suffered and died for us.
In his name, my God, have mercy.

Or:

Lord Jesus,
you chose to be called the friend of sinners.
By your saving death and resurrection

free me from my sins.
May your peace take root in my heart
and bring forth a harvest
of love, holiness, and truth.

Prayer of Thanksgiving

I give you thanks, loving Father, for the gift of your forgiveness. Help me to follow Jesus more closely and during this time of illness to unite my sufferings to his. May your forgiveness bring me health in mind and body. Amen.

COMMUNION

The eucharist is the sacrament of unity. When we receive the eucharist we are united with the risen Lord and with one another. When sickness separates us from our community or our family, the eucharist still unites us.

The familiar term "communion" expresses this oneness with both Jesus and the church. When we receive the eucharistic body of Christ, we are one with his mystical body, the church. Our union with Christ enables us to join our suffering with his self-offering to the Father on the cross. Our union with the church strengthens us because we know we are not alone or forgotten.

Prayer of Preparation

Lord Jesus Christ, your death brought life to the world. May the eucharist I will receive unite me more closely with you and all of my sisters and brothers. May it give me strength of spirit and restore me to health. Amen.

Scripture

> "I am the living bread that came down from heaven. If anyone eats this bread, he will live forever. The bread that I will give is my flesh, which I give so that the world may live" (Jn 6:51).

(You may wish to choose a different scripture reading from Chapter 6 in this book.)

Meditation

Reflect on Jesus' words from this gospel passage: "I am the living bread." Recall his words at the last supper: "This is my body." The eucharist that you will receive truly is the body of Christ, his real presence. Pray repetitively: "Come, Lord Jesus."

Listen again to Jesus' words: "If anyone eats this bread, he will live forever." The eucharist you receive is Jesus' pledge of eternal life; it is his promise that you will one day be whole and fully alive with him. Pray quietly: "Say but the word, and I shall be healed."

Jesus said: "The bread that I will give is my flesh, which I give so that the world may live." When Jesus told us, "Do this in memory of me," he not only meant that we should celebrate the eucharist as a memorial of his death, but that we too should give our flesh, our very selves, for the life of others. Repeat in your heart: "Jesus, bread of life."

Prayer of Thanksgiving

All powerful and ever living God, thank you for the nourishment of this eucharist. Thank you for your presence for me in this time of illness and for all those who care for me. May this communion bring me healing of body and soul. Amen.

ANOINTING OF THE SICK

Jesus frequently showed special concern for the sick, offering them both physical and spiritual healing. Through his presence, his words, and often his touch, he gave them the gift of faith, forgiveness, and bodily health. We know from the letter of St. James that the early church followed the Lord's lead: "Is there anyone who is sick? He should send for the church elders, who will pray for him and rub olive oil on him in the name of the Lord" (Jas 5:14).

Today, Jesus' healing love is available to us through the sacrament of anointing of the sick. In the past it was called "extreme unction" and was associated with the dying. But following the reforms of the Second Vatican Council, we recognize today that the sacrament is for anyone who is seriously ill. Through it Christ strengthens us—alleviating our anxiety, uplifting our spirits, and sometimes fostering our physical health as well.

The sacrament can be received more than once, for example if a person has a recurring illness or a condition worsens. It is often celebrated upon admission to the hospital or before surgery. An elderly person whose condition has worsened may also receive the sacrament, even if there is no diagnosis of serious illness. The celebration includes a reading from the scriptures, a laying on of hands by the priest, and the anointing of the forehead and the hands accompanied by a prayer.

Prayer of Preparation

Lord, you made the blind see, the deaf hear, and the lame walk. Hear me now as I turn to you in my need. I trust that you know my needs better than I myself do. Help me to be open to your healing touch, in my heart, in my soul, in my mind, and in my body. Through this anointing grant me the strength and healing that I need. Amen.

Scripture

> A man suffering from a dreaded skin disease came to Jesus, knelt down, and begged him for help. "If you want to," he said, "you can make me clean." Jesus was filled with pity, and reached out and touched him. "I do want to," he answered. "Be clean!" At once the disease left the man, and he was clean (Mk 1:40-42).

(You may wish to choose a different scripture reading from Chapter 6 in this book.)

Meditation

When Jesus responded to the leper's request in this story, his answer was one of spontaneous love: "I do want to . . . be clean!" To those of us who have been trained to think that sickness, or any form of suffering, is the will of God, such a response can seem like it would never apply to us. Yet this gospel passage and the many other accounts of Jesus' healing give us a sense that God's will can often include our healing.

In St. John's gospel Jesus says: "I have come in order that you might have life—life in all its fullness" (Jn 10:10). Jesus' actions showed what he meant by this fullness of life—forgiveness, healing, and a new relationship with God. These were all a part of his heart's desire for those whom he touched.

Although we may have a tendency to interpret the bad things that happen to us as God's will, we might benefit more from an attitude of openness to God during illness. Instead of asking the question, "Why am I sick?" we might ask, "What does God want to do with me during this time of illness?" This opens us to receive whatever God wishes to give us, whether it be a change of heart about certain things, a deeper awareness of God's place in our lives, or a new sense of direction for the future.

Ask God to open you to understand and accept his heart's desire for you, whatever that might be.

Prayer of Thanksgiving

Loving and merciful God, I offer you thanks for the gift of your healing love. I know that your Holy Spirit is at work in me to strengthen and heal me. Increase my trust in you so that in both sickness and health I can follow you more closely. Amen.

VIATICUM

One of the prayers of the funeral rite reminds us of our ultimate destiny as Christians: "Lord, for your faithful people life is changed, not ended." When we come to the end of our earthly journey, the Lord accompanies us "through the valley of darkness" to his kingdom. Christ is especially present to us through viaticum, the eucharist for the dying.

The word "viaticum" comes from the Latin word meaning "traveling provisions." It is food for our journey and the pledge of our resurrection. Jesus promised us, "Whoever eats my flesh and drinks my blood has eternal life, and I will raise him to life on the last day" (Jn 6:54).

As baptism began our Christian journey, viaticum brings it to its conclusion. Thus, part of the celebration includes the renewal of our baptismal promises. The usual minister of viaticum is the parish priest, although when circumstances require, any priest, deacon, or duly authorized lay person can be the minister.

Viaticum can be received more than once, for example if one recovers from a crisis but then falls back into it or one continues to be in a critical state for some time. Then, viaticum can be received daily.

Prayer of Preparation

Jesus, gentle shepherd, you have been with me throughout my life, leading me and guiding me along the right path. Hear me now as I call on you once again. Be with me as I enter the dark valley of death. Ease my fears, comfort me. Come to me through the sacrament of your body and blood and be my companion on my journey to your kingdom. Let me join you at the heavenly banquet which you have prepared for me. Amen.

Scripture

> "Whoever eats my flesh and drinks my blood has eternal life, and I will raise him to life on the last day. For my flesh is real food; my blood is real drink. Whoever eats my flesh and drinks my blood lives in me, and I live in him" (Jn 6:54-56).

Review of Life

In preparation for viaticum, reflect on your life as a gift from God. Offer your thanks for the gift of faith and for all the blessings you have received. Ask God's pardon for your sins. Pray quietly the prayer of Jesus on the cross: "In your hands I place my spirit!"

Concluding Prayer

Lord Jesus, you are the way, the truth, and the life. Grant me your protection, your comfort, and your peace as I place my life in your care. Amen.

SIX

Jesus' Healing Love

In Jesus, God's love was made flesh. His words, his actions, and particularly the miracles he performed, were signs that God was at work in the world in a new way—offering healing, forgiveness, and new life.

The biblical passages presented here remind us of the healing love of Jesus. In the gospels, Jesus' healings were always accompanied by faith. Sometimes faith led to healing, other times healing created faith. In every case they were expressions of Jesus' love and concern for the sick.

As you read and reflect on these stories and sayings, put yourself in the place of the sick person. Let his or her words be yours. Then listen to Jesus' words as if they were directed to you personally.

JESUS HEALS A ROMAN OFFICER'S SERVANT

When Jesus entered Capernaum, a Roman officer met him and begged for help: "Sir, my servant is sick in bed at home, unable to move and suffering terribly."

"I will go and make him well," Jesus said.

"Oh no, sir," answered the officer. "I do not deserve to have you come into my house. Just give the order, and my servant will get well. I, too, am a man under the authority of superior officers, and I have soldiers under me. I order this one, 'Go!' and he goes; and I order that one, 'Come!' and he comes; and I order my slave, 'Do this!' and he does it."

When Jesus heard this, he was surprised and said to the people following him, "I tell you, I have never found anyone in Israel with faith like this. I assure you that many will come from the east and the west and sit down with Abraham, Isaac, and Jacob at the feast in the Kingdom of heaven. But those who should be in the Kingdom will be thrown out into the darkness, where they will cry and gnash their teeth." Then Jesus said to the officer, "Go home, and what you believe will be done for you."

And the officer's servant was healed that very moment.

—*Matthew 8:5-13*

JESUS HEALS MANY PEOPLE

Jesus went to Peter's home, and there he saw Peter's mother-in-law sick in bed with a fever.

He touched her hand; the fever left her, and she got up and began to wait on him.

When evening came, people brought to Jesus many who had demons in them. Jesus drove out the evil spirits with a word and healed all who were sick. He did this to make come true what the prophet Isaiah had said, "He himself took our sickness and carried away our diseases."

—*Matthew 8:14-17*

JESUS HEALS BLIND BARTIMAEUS

They came to Jericho, and as Jesus was leaving with his disciples and a large crowd, a blind beggar named Bartimaeus son of Timaeus was sitting by the road. When he heard that it was Jesus of Nazareth, he began to shout, "Jesus! Son of David! Have mercy on me!" Many of the people scolded him and told him to be quiet. But he shouted even more loudly, "Son of David, have mercy on me!"

Jesus stopped and said, "Call him." So they called the blind man. "Cheer up!" they said. "Get up, he is calling you." So he threw off his cloak, jumped up, and came to Jesus.

"What do you want me to do for you?" Jesus asked him. "Teacher," the blind man answered, "I want to see again." "Go," Jesus told him, "your faith has made you well." At once he was able to see and followed Jesus on the road.

—*Mark 10:46-52*

ASK AND YOU WILL RECEIVE

Jesus said to his disciples, "Suppose one of you should go to a friend's house at midnight and say to him, 'Friend, let me borrow three loaves of bread. A friend of mine who is on a trip has just come to my house, and I don't have any food for him!' And suppose your friend should answer from inside, 'Don't bother me! The door is already locked, and my children and I are in bed. I can't get up and give you anything.' Well, what then? I tell you that even if he will not get up and give you the bread because you are his friend, yet he will get up and give you everything you need because you are not ashamed to keep on asking.

"And so I say to you: Ask, and you will receive; seek, and you will find; knock, and the door will be opened to you. For everyone who asks will receive, and he who seeks will find, and the door will be opened to anyone who knocks.

"Would any of you who are fathers give your

son a snake when he asks for fish? Or would you give him a scorpion when he asks for an egg? As bad as you are, you know how to give good things to your children. How much more, then, will the Father in heaven give the Holy Spirit to those who ask him!"

—*Luke 11:5-13*

JESUS HEALS A MAN BORN BLIND

As Jesus was walking along, he saw a man who had been born blind. His disciples asked him, "Teacher, whose sin caused him to be born blind? Was it his own or his parents' sin?"

Jesus answered, "His blindness has nothing to do with his sins or his parents' sins. He is blind so that God's power might be seen at work in him. As long as it is day, we must do the work of him who sent me; night is coming when no one can work. While I am in the world, I am the light for the world."

After he said this, Jesus spat on the ground and made some mud with the spittle; he rubbed the mud on the man's eyes and told him, "Go and wash your face in the Pool of Siloam." (This name means "Sent.") So the man went, washed his face, and came back seeing.

—*John 9:1-7*

COME TO ME AND REST

"Come to me, all of you who are tired from carrying heavy loads, and I will give you rest. Take my yoke and put it on you, and learn from me, because I am gentle and humble in spirit; and you will find rest. For the yoke I will give you is easy, and the load I will put on you is light."

—*Matthew 11:28-30*

JAIRUS' DAUGHTER AND THE WOMAN WHO TOUCHED JESUS' CLOAK

Jesus went back across to the other side of the lake. There at the lakeside a large crowd gathered around him. Jairus, an official of the local synagogue, arrived, and when he saw Jesus, he threw himself down at his feet and begged him earnestly, "My little daughter is very sick. Please come and place your hands on her, so that she will get well and live!"

Then Jesus started off with him. So many people were going along with Jesus that they were crowding him from every side.

There was a woman who had suffered terribly from severe bleeding for twelve years, even though she had been treated by many doctors. She had spent all her money, but instead of getting better she got worse all the time. She had heard about Jesus, so she came in the crowd behind him, saying to herself, "If I just touch his clothes, I will get well."

She touched his cloak, and her bleeding stopped at once; and she had the feeling inside herself that she was healed of her trouble. At once Jesus knew that power had gone out of him, so he turned around in the crowd and asked, "Who touched my clothes?"

His disciples answered, "You see how the people are crowding you; why do you ask who touched you?"

But Jesus kept looking around to see who had done it. The woman realized what had happened to her, so she came, trembling with fear, knelt at his feet, and told him the whole truth. Jesus said to her, "My daughter, your faith has made you well. Go in peace, and be healed of your trouble."

While Jesus was saying this, some messengers came from Jairus' house and told him, "Your daughter has died. Why bother the Teacher any longer?"

Jesus paid no attention to what they said, but told him, "Don't be afraid, only believe." Then he did not let anyone else go on with him except Peter and James and his brother

John. They arrived at Jairus' house, where Jesus saw the confusion and heard all the loud crying and wailing. He went in and said to them, "Why all this confusion? Why are you crying? The child is not dead—she is only sleeping!"

They started making fun of him, so he put them all out, took the child's father and mother and his three disciples, and went into the room where the child was lying. He took her by the hand and said to her, "*Talitha, koum*," which means, "Little girl, I tell you to get up!"

She got up at once and started walking around. (She was twelve years old.) When this happened, they were completely amazed. But Jesus gave them strict orders not to tell anyone, and he said, "Give her something to eat."

—*Mark 5:21-43*

CARRYING THE CROSS DAILY

And he said to them all, "If anyone wants to come with me, he must forget himself, take up his cross every day, and follow me. For whoever wants to save his own life will lose it, but whoever loses his life for my sake will save it. Will a person gain anything if he wins the whole world but is himself lost or defeated? Of course not!"

—*Luke 9:23-25*

JESUS HEALS A PARALYZED MAN

One day when Jesus was teaching, some Pharisees and teachers of the Law were sitting there who had come from every town in Galilee and Judea and from Jerusalem. The power of the Lord was present for Jesus to heal the sick. Some men came carrying a paralyzed man on a bed, and they tried to carry him into the house and put him in front of Jesus. Because of the crowd, however, they could find no way to take him in. So they carried him up on the roof, made an opening in the tiles, and let him down on his bed into the middle of the group in front of Jesus. When Jesus saw how much faith they had, he said to the man, "Your sins are forgiven, my friend."

The teachers of the Law and the Pharisees began to say to themselves, "Who is this man who speaks such blasphemy! God is the only one who can forgive sins!"

Jesus knew their thoughts and said to them, "Why do you think such things? Is it easier to say 'Your sins are forgiven you,' or to say, 'Get up and walk'? I will prove to you, then, that the Son of Man has authority on earth to forgive sins." So he said to the paralyzed man, "I tell you, get up, pick up your bed, and go home!"

At once the man got up in front of them all, took the bed he had been lying on, and went home, praising God. They were all completely amazed! Full of fear, they praised God, saying, "What marvelous things we have seen today!"

—Luke 5:17-26

TRUST IN GOD

Then Jesus said to the disciples, "And so I tell you not to worry about the food you need to stay alive or about the clothes you need for your body. Life is much more important than food, and the body much more important than clothes. Look at the crows: they don't plant seeds or gather a harvest; they don't have storage rooms or barns; God feeds them! You are worth so much more than birds! Can any of you live a bit longer by worrying about it?"

—Luke 12:22-25

SEVEN

Short Meditations

All of us struggle to find God, whether we are well or ill. We all have questions, fears, and uncertainties. Perhaps these reflections and meditations will help you to find God during this period of your life.

ONE SET OF FOOTPRINTS

One night a man had a dream. He dreamed he was walking along the beach with the Lord. Across the sky flashed scenes from his life. For each scene he noticed two sets of footprints in the sand—one belonging to him, the other to the Lord.

When the last scene of his life flashed before him, he looked back at the footprints in the sand, and he noticed that many times along the path of his life there was only one set of footprints. He also noticed that it happened at the very lowest and saddest times in his life.

This really bothered him, and he questioned the Lord about it. "Lord, you said that once I decided to follow you, you'd walk with me all the way. But I've noticed that during the most difficult times in my life, there is only one set of footprints. I don't understand why in times when I needed you most, you would leave me."

The Lord replied: "My precious, precious child. I love you and I would never, never leave you during your trials and suffering. When you see only one set of footprints, it was then that I carried you!"

—*Anonymous*

GOD WILL TAKE CARE OF YOU

Be not dismayed whate'er betide,
God will take care of you;
beneath his wings of love abide,
God will take care of you.

No matter what may be the test,
God will take care of you;
lean, weary one, upon his breast,
God will take care of you.

God will take care of you,
through every day, o'er all the way;
he will take care of you,
God will take care of you.

—*Methodist Hymn*

NO PRAYER IS WASTED

Scripture tells us "prayer made in faith will heal the sick person" (Jas 5:15). Yet all of us can doubtless recall times—many times—when we prayed for a healing and it did not occur. . . . Does that mean that God is not listening? That your faith is too weak? Or that your prayers have not been fervent enough? I think not, but I also think it is fruitless to try to find an answer to why some people are healed and some are not.

Much of what happens on our earthly journey will remain a mystery until we get to risen life. . . . I do not think we can ever say prayer is wasted. Although prayer may not change a situation and give us the miracle we want, *prayer changes us*. Through prayer, we become more aware of God's presence. Through prayer, we find inner resources and strength we didn't know we had. Through prayer, we are no longer facing our fears and pain alone: God is beside us, renewing our spirit, restoring our soul, and helping us carry the burden when it becomes too heavy for us to bear alone.

—Ron DelBene

AT THE LORD'S FEAST

My understanding was lifted up into heaven, where I saw our Lord like a lord in his own house who has called all his valued servants and friends to a solemn feast . . . and [Christ] filled [the house] with joy and mirth. He himself endlessly gladdened and solaced his valued friends . . . with the marvelous melody of endless love in his own fair, blessed face. This glorious countenance of the godhead completely fills all heaven with joy and bliss. . . .

God showed three degrees of bliss that every soul that has willingly served God . . . shall have in heaven. The first is gratitude . . . he shall receive from our Lord God. . . . The second is that all the blessed creatures who are in heaven shall see the glorious thanking. . . . The third is that it shall last forever.

—Blessed Julian of Norwich

MY HOUSE BY THE SEA

I built my house by the sea.
Not on the sands, mind you,
not on the shifting sand.
And I built it of rock.
A strong house
by a strong sea.
And we got well-acquainted, the sea and I.
Good neighbors.

Not that we spoke much.
We met in silences,
respectful, keeping our distance
but looking our thoughts across the fence
of sand.
Always the fence of sand our barrier,
always the sand between.
And then one day
(and I still don't know how it happened)
The sea came.
Without warning.
Without welcome even.
Not sudden and swift, but a shifting across
the sand like wine.
Less like the flow of water than the flow of
blood.
Slow, but flowing like an open wound.
And I thought of flight, and I thought of
drowning, and I thought of death.
But while I thought the sea crept higher till
it reached my door.
And I knew that there was neither flight nor
death nor drowning.
That when the sea comes calling you stop
being good neighbors,
well-acquainted, friendly from a distance
neighbors.
And you give your house for a coral castle
and you learn to breathe under water.

—*Carol Bialock*

ABANDONMENT

What is an abandonment experience?
Is it leaving oneself on God's doorstep,
walking into the rest of life,
not allowing anxiety,
fear, frustration to enter into one?
Is it expecting God to keep one warm,
secure, and safe, unharmed?
Is that abandonment?

Abandonment has nothing to do with warmth
or womb or arms or close clasped hearts.
It is not something done by a child.
It is done to him.
It cannot be done to an adult.
It is done by him.
Abandonment is committed only with and
in the maturity of Christ Jesus.
It is not just a hanging loose.
It is a letting go.
It is a severing of the strings by which one
manipulates, controls, administrates the
forces in one's life.
Abandonment is receiving all things the way
one receives a gift
with opened hands,
an opened heart.
Abandonment to God
is the climactic point in any [person's] life.

—*Anonymous*

THE POTTER

The woman potter summarized not only the making of a pot but her basic belief about life:

> Both my hands shaped this pot. And, the place where it actually forms is a place of tension between the pressure applied from the outside and the pressure of the hand on the inside. That's the way my life has been. Sadness and death and misfortune and the love of friends and all the things that happened to me that I didn't even choose. All of that influenced my life. But, there are things I believe in about myself, my faith in God and the love of some friends that worked on the insides of me. My life, like this pot, is the result of what happened on the outside and what was going on inside of me. Life, like this pot, comes to be in places of tension. Life comes to be when we learn how to avoid looking for answers and finally learn how to ask the questions that will bring us to life.

There is a tendency in us to want to live tension-free. But, like the woman potter, I believe that this tension is God's gift to us, a gift that sometimes will not permit us to escape its presence. I believe that our creative energies are activated by just that kind of upsetting tension. It is in responding to this gnawing discomfort that we have the possibility of giving shape to dreams that are at once faithful to who we are and who we can become.

—*Paula Ripple*

A KISS OF JESUS

Suffering—pain, humiliation, sickness, and failure—is but a kiss of Jesus.

Once I met a lady who had a terrible cancer. She was suffering so much. I told her, "Now you come so close to Jesus on the cross that he is kissing you." Then she joined hands and said, "Mother Teresa, please tell Jesus to stop kissing me."

It was so beautiful. She understood. Suffering is a gift of God, a gift that makes us Christlike. People must not accept suffering as a punishment.

—*Mother Teresa*

Additional Acknowledgments and Sources

"The Potter" is from *Growing Strong at Broken Places* by Paula Ripple, copyright © 1986 by Ave Maria Press, Notre Dame, IN. Used by permission.

"A Kiss of Jesus" is from *Words to Love By* by Mother Teresa © 1983 by Ave Maria Press, Notre Dame, IN. Used by permission.

"In Time of Sickness," "Your Will Be Done," "Lord Jesus, Healer," and "In Time of Serious Illness" are reprinted from *Lord Hear Our Prayer,* edited by William G. Storey and Thomas McNally, copyright © 1978, Ave Maria Press, Notre Dame, IN. Used by permission.

"Prayer for Strength of Spirit" by Valerie Lesniak, CSJ, "Prayer Before Surgery," "Prayer Following Surgery," "Prayer When Suffering Pain," and "Prayer on Recovery from Illness" are reprinted with permission of St. Joseph Medical Center, South Bend, IN. All rights reserved.

"Behold, Jesus," originally titled "Healing," is reprinted from *Celtic Fire*, edited by Robert van de Weyer, copyright © 1990, Doubleday Publishing, New York.

Psalm 42 and Psalm 131 are from the revised *Psalms of The New American Bible*, Collegeville, MN: The Liturgical Press, 1991.

Psalm 121 is from *The New Jerusalem Bible*, New York: Doubleday & Company, 1985.

Psalm 91 is from *Psalms Anew: In Inclusive Language* by Nancy Schreck and Maureen Leach, Winona, MN: St. Mary's Press, 1986.

Psalm 23 and Psalm 63 are from *The Grail Psalter*, The Grail (England), London: Collins, 1963.

Psalm 27, Psalm 31, and Psalm 138 are from *The New Revised Standard Version*, New York: Oxford University Press, 1991.

"Abandonment" is quoted from *Disciples and Other Strangers* by Edward Farrell, Dimension Books, Denville, NJ.

"No Prayer Is Wasted" is from *Near Life's End* by Ron DelBene with Mary and Herb Montgomery, Nashville, TN: The Upper Room, 1988.

"My House By the Sea" by Carol Bialock is

reprinted from *Good Friday People* by Shiela Cassidy, Maryknoll, NY: Orbis Books, 1991.

Any prayer not credited is by the author. If through inadvertence proper credit has not been given to the author of any prayer, please inform the publisher who will make the correction in the next edition of the book.